A STATEMENT

OF THE

THEORY OF EDUCATION

IN

THE UNITED STATES OF AMERICA,

AS APPROVED BY

MANY LEADING EDUCATORS.

WASHINGTON:
GOVERNMENT PRINTING OFFICE.
1874.

LETTER

OF THE

COMMISSIONER OF EDUCATION.

LETTER.

DEPARTMENT OF THE INTERIOR,
BUREAU OF EDUCATION,
Washington, D. C., December 15, 1874.

SIR: A meeting of State-superintendents and others was held in Washington, November 13, 1872, to make preliminary arrangements for the representation at Vienna of the condition of education in the United States. A full report of this meeting will be found in the Circular of Information of this Bureau for November, 1872, pages 29–40.

At this meeting, it was resolved (see page 36 of the circular above referred to) "that we consider it exceedingly desirable that there should be a brief statement, embodying clearly the idea of the relation of the American free school to the American Commonwealth; and we recommend to the Commissioner of Education that such a statement shall be prepared as can be signed generally by the educators of the country as a declaration of their sentiments."

The preparation of this statement was intrusted to Hon. Duane Doty, superintendent of city-schools, Detroit, Mich. In conjunction with Hon. W. T. Harris, superintendent of city-schools, Saint Louis, Mo., he prepared a statement, which was subsequently submitted to the several leading educators whose names are hereto affixed in witness of their approval of the statement.

Although this was not prepared and agreed upon in time to be used at Vienna, yet, in view of the constant demands made upon this Bureau, especially by foreign investigators, for a statement of the school-system in this country; and in view of the natural tendency of such foreigners to fall into the error of supposing that there *is* a national system of education under control of the General Government of the United States; and, moreover, in consideration of the dangers that have been and are threatening the welfare of the free public-school-systems of many of the States, a clear statement of such fundamental principles as all American educators can agree upon seems most timely, as furnishing to the friends of education everywhere a ready means of refuting the false assertions of those who oppose the establishment and prosperity of the schools in their several localities.

The free public education of the children of the United States depends everywhere upon the action taken by the several States and by the citizens of those States in their several localities. The existence of a republic, unless all its citizens are educated, is an admitted impossibility. The school-systems of many States have suffered from the results of the war; and their speedy and healthy advancement to the greatest efficiency possible is, therefore, of vital interest to the whole country.

For the above reasons and as a matter of great convenience to this Office in replying to constant demands for such information, I recommend the printing of this statement.

Very respectfully, your obedient servant,

JOHN EATON,
Commissioner.

Hon. C. DELANO,
Secretary of the Interior.

Approved and publication ordered.

B. R. COWEN,
Acting Secretary.

STATEMENT

OF THE

THEORY OF EDUCATION

IN

THE UNITED STATES.

A STATEMENT OF THE THEORY OF EDUCATION IN THE UNITED STATES OF AMERICA.

I.

The American school-system is an organic or historic growth, having its origin in attempts made to supply social and political needs.

II.

By the Constitution of the United States, no powers are vested in the central Government of the nation, unless the same relate immediately to the support and defense of the whole people, to their intercourse with foreign powers, or to the subordination of the several States composing the Union. Military education for the Army and Navy only has been directly provided for by the national Government; and the further action in aid of education has been limited to endowments in the form of land-grants to the several States, or portions thereof, for the purpose of providing a fund for the support of common schools or to found colleges for the promotion of scientific agriculture and the mechanic arts. Universities also have been endowed by the United States Government in all the new States since the Northwest Territory was organized in 1787. Recently, (in 1867,) a Bureau of Education has been established at the seat of Government and a national Commissioner appointed, who collects statistics and disseminates valuable information relating to all educational subjects. To the several States individually is left, for the most part, the local administration of justice, as well as the establishment of public agencies for the well-being of the civil and social community in its industrial, economical, social, and spiritual aspects.

III.

The general form of the national Government is largely copied in the civil organization of the particular States, and no powers or functions of an administrative character are ordinarily exercised by the State as a whole which concern only the particular interests and well-being of the subordinate organizations or corporations into which

the State is divided for judicial and municipal purposes; but the State usually vests these local powers and functions in the corporations themselves, such as counties, townships, and cities. The power of the State over these local corporations is complete; but they are generally allowed large legislative and administrative powers of a purely local character, while the State ordinarily confines its action and legislation to matters in which the people of the whole State are interested.

IV.

Citizenship in the nation is defined by Articles XIV and XV of Amendments to the Constitution, and is uniform, including every native and all naturalized persons. The right of voting and holding office is not inherent in citizenship, but is given to such as the States or the General Government determine, except that neither race nor color can be allowed as a test. Each State-constitution defines the qualifications necessary for the exercise of the political functions of holding office in the civil government and electing the citizens who are to fill such offices. The State, in its entire existence, is a reflex of the people thus defined as its electors. In their hands collectively is vested the ultimate responsibility for all the power which is expressed through the organism of the State, or, less directly, through the nation itself. Upon the several States individually, in which is vested the power of defining the qualifications of the electors who choose by ballot the representatives that make and execute the laws of the land, rests the responsibility of making provision for the education of those charged with the primary political functions. This responsibility has been generally recognized in the establishment, by legislative enactment, of a system of free common schools, supported in part by State-school-funds accumulated from national grants of lands and from appropriations made from the State-revenue, and in part by local taxation or assessment made upon those directly benefited by the schools themselves. The local direction and management of the schools are left to the municipalities or to the local corporate bodies organized for the special purpose, and a general supervision is reserved to itself by the State. In some States, compulsory educational laws have been passed; not, however, requiring those who are taught in other ways to resort to the public schools.

The State arranges the school-system and designates the various kinds of schools to be supported and managed by the public authorities and sometimes prescribes more or less of the branches of knowledge to be taught; provides how districts may be created, divided, or consolidated with others and how moneys may be raised by or for

them; prescribes their organization, officers and their powers, and the time and manner of filling and vacating offices and the functions of each officer; prescribes the school-age and conditions of attendance; and provides in some cases for the investment and application of the school-funds derived from the General Government. The local municipalities organize school-districts under State-laws, elect school-officers, and levy and collect taxes for school-purposes. The local school-officers examine, appoint, and fix the salaries of teachers when not otherwise done, build school-houses, procure school-supplies, arrange courses of study, prescribe the rules and regulations for the government of the schools, and administer the schools.

V.

By the definitions before referred to, the privilege of political participation in choosing those who administer the government of the country is conferred upon the people at large, with certain general limitations as to sex and age and certain specific limitations regarding the naturalization of aliens (and, until recently, in some States, regarding race or color) or the possession of property or intelligence, &c. The general participation of all the people in the primary political functions of election, together with the almost complete localization of self-government by local administration, renders necessary the education of all, without distinction of sex, social rank, wealth, or natural abilities. This position is generally recognized in theory and practice.

VI.

In proportion to its degree of localization, the administration of the government becomes charged with the interests of civil society, and thus directly concerned in the creation and distribution of wealth and the personal well-being of the individual in the community. The national Government and the State-governments regard education as a proper subject for legislation, on the ground of the necessity of educated intelligence among a people that is to furnish *law-abiding citizens*, well versed in the laws they are to obey, and likewise *law-making citizens*, well versed in the social, historic, and political conditions which give occasion to new laws and shape their provisions. But the municipal or local corporations, in which are vested the direct control and management of educational institutions and the collection and disbursement of the funds necessary for their support, regard education in its social and economic aspects as well as in the more general one of its political function. Hence, all communities, in their local capacity, exceed the limits prescribed by the State in their provisions for popular education, and they do this in the ratio of their grade of advancement in wealth and social culture. The productive industry of the community is known to have a direct relation to the diffusion of educated intelligence therein.

VII.

The idea of the state and the idea of civil society—the former the idea of the actualization of justice and the latter that of the supply of human wants and necessities through the creation and distribution of wealth—conspire, by general consent, in the production of the American system of public education; and, to its maintenance and support, the property of the community is made to contribute by taxation. Both the preservation of property by the actualization of justice and the increase of property by productive industry are directly conditioned, in a republic, upon the educated intelligence of the people. This is so, especially in that species of incorporeal property of the nature of franchises, such as constitute the basis of those corporate combinations formed for the promotion of manufactures and commerce, the creation of transit-facilities, and the diffusion of information, (patent-rights, charters for railroads, canals, telegraphs, banks of issue, insurance-companies, &c.) These franchises, vested in corporations, incite to the production of wealth to an extraordinary degree, and at the same time make such a demand upon the community for directive intelligence that it may be said that the modern industrial community cannot exist without free popular education carried out in a system of schools ascending from the primary grade to the university. And without a free development of productive industry, enabling the individual to accumulate the wealth necessary for the supply of the necessities of life faster than he consumes them, there is not left the leisure requisite to that cultivation of intelligence needed in the theoretical discussion and comprehension of public affairs; and without such occupation of the individual with public affairs, a democracy could exist only in name.

VIII.

The past and present history of the United States exhibits a process of development comprising three stages:

(*a*) The settlement of new territory by pioneers and the reduction of the wilderness to an agricultural country.

(*b*) The rise of commercial towns and the creation of transit-facilities in the new regions.

(*c*) The development of manufacturing centers and the ascendency of domestic commerce.

In consequence of this constant spectacle of the entire process of founding a civilization and developing it from the rudimentary stages up to the completed type, there is produced a peculiar phase of character in the American people. There is always unlimited opportunity for the individual to build anew his fortunes when disaster has overtaken him in one locality.

As a consequence of the perpetual migration from the older sections of the country to the unoccupied Territories, there are new States in all degrees of formation, and their institutions present earlier phases of realization of the distinctive type than are presented in the mature growth of the system as it exists in the thickly-settled and older States. Thus States are to be found with little or no provision for education, but they are rudimentary forms of the American State, and are adopting, as rapidly as immigration enables them to do so, the type of educational institutions already defined as the result of the American political and social ideas.

IX.

The education of the people in schools is a phase of education lying between the earliest period of family-nurture, which is still a concomitant and powerful auxiliary, on the one hand, and the necessary initiation into the specialties of a vocation in practical life on the other. In America, the peculiarities of civil society and the political organization draw the child out of the influence of family-nurture earlier than is common in other countries. The frequent separation of the younger branches of the family from the old stock renders family-influence less powerful in molding character. The consequence of this is the increased importance of the school in an ethical point of view.

X.

In order to compensate for lack of family-nurture, the school is obliged to lay more stress upon discipline and to make far more prominent the moral phase of education. It is obliged to train the pupil into habits of prompt obedience to his teachers and the practice of self-control in its various forms, in order that he may be prepared for a life wherein there is little police-restraint on the part of the constituted authorities.

XI.

The school-discipline, in its phase of substitute for the family, uses *corrective* punishment, which presupposes a feeble development of the sense of honor in the child. It is mostly corporal punishment. But in the phase wherein the school performs the function of preparing the pupil for the formal government of the state, it uses *retributive* punishment and suspends the pupil from some or all the privileges of the school. In this phase of discipline, a sense of honor is presupposed and strengthened.

XII.

In commercial cities and towns, the tendency preponderates towards forms of punishment founded on the sense of honor and towards the entire disuse of corporal punishment. This object has been successfully accomplished in New York, Chicago, Syracuse, and some other cities. In the schools of the country, where the agricultural interest prevails, the tendency to the family-form of government is marked.

XIII.

A further difference between the discipline of city-schools and that of country-schools is founded partly on the fact that the former schools are usually quite large, assembling from three hundred to fifteen hundred pupils in one building, while the latter have commonly less than fifty pupils. In the former, the large numbers admit of good classification; in the latter, classes are quite small, sometimes containing only a single pupil, and the discipline of combination is consequently feebly developed. The commercial tone prevalent in the city tends to develop, in its schools, quick, alert habits and readiness to combine with others in their tasks. Military precision is required in the maneuvering of classes. Great stress is laid upon (1) punctuality, (2) regularity, (3) attention, and (4) silence, as habits necessary through life for successful combination with one's fellow-men in an industrial and commercial civilization.

XIV.

The course of study is laid down with a view to giving the pupil the readiest and most thorough practical command of those conventionalities of intelligence, those arts and acquirements which are the means of directive power and of further self-education. These preliminary educational accomplishments open at once to the mind of the pupil two opposite directions: (*a*) the immediate mastery ove the material world, for the purposes of obtaining food, clothing, and shelter directly; (*b*) the initiation into the means of association with one's fellow-men, the world of humanity.

XV.

(*a*) The first theoretical study necessary for the mastery over the material world is arithmetic—the quantification of objects as regards numbers.

In American schools, this is looked upon as of so much importance that more time is given to it than to any other study of the course. Its cultivation of the habit of attention and accuracy is especially valued.

After arithmetic follows geography, in a parallel direction, looking towards natural history. Arithmetic is taught from the first entrance into school, while geography is begun as soon as the pupil can read well.

XVI.

(*b*) The first theoretical study necessary to facilitate combination of man with his fellow-men is reading the printed page. Accordingly, the prevailing custom in American schools is to place a book in the hands of the child when he first enters school and to begin his instruction with teaching him how to read. As soon as he can read, he is able to begin to learn to study books for himself, and thus to acquire stores of knowledge by his own efforts. The art of writing is learned in connection with reading. This culture, in the direction of knowing the feelings, sentiments, and ideas of mankind, is continued throughout the course by a graded series of readers, containing selections of the gems from the literature of the language, both prose and verse. This culture is re-enforced about the fifth year of the course by the study of English grammar, in which, under a thin veil, the pupil learns to discern the categories of the mind and to separate them analytically from modifying surroundings and define them. The common forms of thought and of its expression are thus mastered, and in this way the pupil is to some extent initiated into pure thought and acquires the ability to resolve problems of the material world and of his own life into their radical elements. The study of the history of the United States (and, in most instances, of the national Constitution) carries on this culture by the contemplation of the peculiarities of his nation as exhibited in its historic relations.

XVII.

The cardinal studies of the "common school" are: (1) reading and writing, (2) grammar, (3) arithmetic, (4) geography; the first two look towards mastery over spiritual combination; the latter two, over material combination. The common school aims to give the pupil the great arts of receiving and communicating intelligence. Drawing and vocal music are taught quite generally and the rudiments of natural science are taught orally in most city-schools. Declamation of oratorical selections is a favorite exercise and is supposed to fit the youth for public and political life. Debating societies are formed for the same purpose.

XVIII.

The secondary education, carried on in "high schools," "academies," and "seminaries," to the studies of the common school adds: (1) on the side of the theoretical command of material means: (*a*) algebra, geometry, calculus, and some forms of engineering, (surveying, navigation, &c.;) (*b*) natural philosophy or physics, (*i. e.*, nature quantitatively considered;) (*c*) physical geography or natural history, (nature organically considered.) (2) On the side of the humanities: (*a*) rhetoric, (*b*) English literature, (*c*) Latin, (the basis of the English vocabulary, as regards generalization and reflection as well as social refinement,) (*d*) a modern language, commonly German or French, of which the latter serves the same general purpose as Latin in giving to English-speaking people a readier command, a more intuitive sense of the meaning of the vocabulary of words contributed by the Roman civilization to modern languages, and especially to the English, (whose vocabulary is chiefly Roman, though its grammatical form is Gothic.)

The high schools generally form a portion of the free public-school-system; the academies and seminaries are generally founded and supported by private enterprise or religious zeal, and are not controlled or interfered with by the State, although many of them are chartered by it and are free from taxation.

XIX.

The highest form of school-education is found in the colleges and universities scattered through the country, some under the control and support of the State, but far the larger number founded and supported by religious denominations or private endowment and tuition-fees from the students. All, or nearly all, of them are chartered by the State, and their property is exempt from taxation. These institutions support one or more of the following courses:

(*a*) Academic course, generally of four years, a continuation of the secondary education, as herein described, embracing a course in Latin and Greek, French and German, higher mathematics and some of their applications, the general technics of the natural sciences and also of the social and political sciences, belles-lettres and universal history, logic, metaphysics, and moral philosophy; (*b*) a scientific school; (*c*) a law-school; (*d*) a medical school; (*e*) a theological seminary; (*f*) a normal school, (for the training of teachers; this is seldom found except in State-universities, but is usually a separate institution, founded by the State or municipality.)

The academic course is the college-course proper; when united to the others, it forms a "university."

XX.

The general system of instruction lays special emphasis on the use of text-books and the prevalent tendency is towards giving the pupil an initiation into the method of using the printed page in the form of books and periodicals for the purpose of obtaining information from the recorded experience of his fellow-men; but in many schools and systems of schools equal or greater stress is laid upon the practical method of conducting investigations for the purpose of verification and of original discovery.

XXI.

In the Northern States, the colored population (being small in number) usually attends the same schools as the white population. In those States in which the colored people are very numerous, separate schools, with few exceptions, are established for them.

XXII.

In the country, girls and boys attend the same school; in some of the older cities, the sexes are educated together in the primary schools, but separated in the grammar- and high schools. The course of study is generally the same for boys and girls. In cities of most recent growth, the co-education of the sexes prevails from the primary school up through the higher grades, and some colleges admit both sexes. There are, also, colleges established for the education of women alone.

XXIII.

Private schools, supported by individual enterprise or by corporations and religious denominations, are numerous, and the course of study in them is nearly the same as in the public schools, except in laying more stress upon certain ornamental branches, such as vocal and instrumental music, French, drawing and painting, embroidery, &c.

These schools are more frequently for the separate education of the sexes and for secondary education. Very many academies and seminaries have been founded with a view to supplying the Christian ministry with clergymen. There are some denominations more or less hostile to the public-school-system because of its secularity, and these favor a division of the school-funds so as to allow each denomination to carry on its own school-system.

XXIV.

Sectarian instruction is not given in the public schools. Religious, particularly sectarian, training is accomplished mainly in families and by the several denominations in their Sunday-schools or in special classes that recite their catechisms at stated intervals during the week. It is quite a common practice to open or close the public schools with Bible-reading and prayer. Singing of religious hymns by the entire school is still more common.

XXV.

Free evening-schools are common in cities, to provide means of improvement for adults and for youths who are prevented from attending the day-schools by reason of some useful employment. Special attention is given in them to reading, writing, arithmetic, and to certain industrial studies, such as book-keeping, line-drawing, &c.

XXVI.

Schools for unfortunates, including reform-schools for vicious children, asylums for the blind, insane, deaf and dumb, idiots, and orphans, are usually established by the State-government directly, and less frequently by municipal corporations, and to some extent by religious denominations. In cities, truant-schools, established by the municipal authorities, are becoming common, and seem to be necessary where compulsory-attendance-laws exist.

XXVII.

In the city-schools, female teachers largely preponderate, composing frequently 90 per cent. of the entire corps of teachers. In country-schools, the proportion is very much smaller, but has increased considerably in late years. The pupil, coming directly from home-influence, finds a less abrupt change upon entering the school under the charge of a female teacher. The female character, being trained by experience in family-supervision to the administration of special details wherein division of labor cannot prevail to any great extent, is eminently fitted to control and manage the education of the child while it is in a state of transition from caprice to rationally-regulated exercise of the will; and the development of individuality is generally more harmonious up to a certain age if the pupil is placed under female teachers. The comparatively small cost of female-labor, also, largely determines its employment in all public schools.

XXVIII.

The ratio of the entire population in school varies from 16 per cent. in some cities down to 5 per cent., or even 3 per cent., in some agricultural sections. City-schools generally hold their sessions daily—from 9 to 12 a.m. and from 1 to 4 p.m., with a recess of a quarter of an hour in each session—for five days in the week, and for about ten months in the year, two months or less being allowed for vacations. In some cities, the plan of half-day-schools for young children has been tried and in many cities such children are not confined to the school-room more than four hours a day. The school-age of the pupil generally begins at 6 years and ends at 16, but in the cooler climates of the northern sections it begins earlier and lasts longer; the school-sessions are usually longer in the colder climates.

XXIX.

The salaries paid teachers indicate somewhat the estimate placed upon their work by the public. For some years there has been a steady increase in salaries. Better qualifications have been brought to the work, and teaching, particularly in cities, has become a regular occupation. Teachers mingle freely in the best social circles and enjoy the respect of the community.

XXX.

Educational journals are published in nearly every State. These journals are sometimes published by the State-superintendent of public instruction, sometimes by committees appointed by State-associations of teachers, and more frequently by individuals. In addition to these periodicals, there are many local educational papers issued by city- or county-teachers' associations, and some of the secular papers have educational departments. The State and city educational reports take rank among the ablest of our public documents.

SIGNATURES.

The foregoing statement is approved by the following gentlemen:

Hon. J. V. Campbell, *Chief justice of Michigan.*

Hon. C. I. Walker, *Law-department of the Michigan University.*

Hon. D. B. Briggs, *State-superintendent, Lansing, Michigan.*

Henry Chaney, *Superintendent of the Detroit Public Library.*

I. M. Wellington, *Principal of the High School, Detroit.*

J. B. Angell, *President of the Michigan University.*

Prof. J. H. Twombly, *President of the Wisconsin University.*

Asa D. Smith, *President of Dartmouth College.*

M. Hopkins, *President of Williams College.*

J. L. Chamberlain, *President of Bowdoin College.*

S. G. Brown, *President of Hamilton College.*

W. A. Stearns, *President of Amherst College.*

Joseph Cummings, *President of the Wesleyan University.*

H. D. Kitchell, *President of Middlebury College.*

Alexis Caswell, *President of Brown University.*

A. D. White, *President of Cornell University.*

W. H. Campbell, *President of Rutgers College.*

Abner Jackson, *President of Trinity College.*

J. C. Burroughs, *President of Chicago University.*

J. M. Gregory, *President of the Illinois Industrial University.*

Hon. Warren Johnson, *State-superintendent of the common schools, Augusta, Maine.*

Hon. J. H. French, *Secretary of the board of education, Burlington, Vermont.*

Hon. Joseph White, *Secretary of the State-board of education, Boston, Massachusetts.*

Hon. B. G. Northrop, *Secretary of the State-board of education, New Haven, Connecticut.*

Hon. A. B. Weaver, *State-superintendent of public instruction, Albany, New York.*

Hon. E. A. Apgar, *State-superintendent of public instruction, Trenton, New Jersey.*

Hon. J. P. Wickersham, *State-superintendent of public instruction, Harrisburg, Pennsylvania.*

Hon. Thomas W. Harvey, *State-commissioner of common schools, Columbus, Ohio.*

Hon. A. C. Shortridge, *Superintendent of city-schools, Indianapolis, Indiana.*

Hon. WILLIAM KEMPT, *Troy, New York.*

Hon. A. P. MARBLE, *Superintendent of city-schools, Worcester, Massachusetts.*

Hon. E. B. HALE, *Superintendent of city-schools, Cambridge, Massachusetts.*

Hon. S. C. HOSFORD, *Superintendent of city-schools, Paterson, New Jersey.*

Hon. G. E. HOOD, *Superintendent of city-schools, Lawrence, Massachusetts.*

ALEXANDER WINCHELL, *President of Syracuse University, New York.*

J. T. CHAMPLIN, *President of Olivet College, Michigan.*

DANIEL READ, *President of the University of Missouri, Columbia, Missouri.*

General A. S. WEBB, *President of the College of the City of New York, New York.*

F. A. P. BARNARD, *President of Columbia College, New York, New York.*

M. B. ANDERSON, *President of Rochester University, Rochester, New York.*

E. N. POTTER, *President of Union College, Schenectady, New York.*

S. HOWARD, *President of the Ohio University, Athens, Ohio.*

E. T. TAPPAN, *President of Kenyon College, Gambier, Ohio.*

O. N. HARTSHORN, *President of Mount Union College, Ohio.*

J. H. FAIRCHILD, *President of Oberlin College, Ohio.*

J. C. WELLING, *President of the Columbia College, Washington, District of Columbia.*

J. H. RAYMOND, *President of Vassar College, Poughkeepsie, New York.*

Hon. M. B. HOPKINS, *State-superintendent of public instruction, Indianapolis, Indiana.*

Hon. SAMUEL FALLOWS, *State-superintendent of public instruction, Madison, Wisconsin.*

Hon. ALONZO ABERNETHY, *State-superintendent of public instruction, Des Moines, Iowa.*

Hon. JOHN MONTEITH, *State-superintendent of public schools, Jefferson City, Missouri.*

Hon. NEWTON BATEMAN, *State-superintendent of public instruction, Springfield, Illinois.*

Hon. H. D. McCARTY, *State-superintendent of public instruction, Leavenworth, Kansas.*

Hon. H. B. WILSON, *State-superintendent of public instruction, Saint Paul, Minnesota.*

Hon. M. A. NEWELL, *Principal of the State Normal School, Baltimore, Maryland.*

Hon. E. E. WHITE, *Editor of the National Teacher, Columbus, Ohio.*

Hon. JOHN D. PHILBRICK, *Superintendent of city-schools, Boston, Massachusetts.*

Hon. W. T. HARRIS, *Superintendent of city-schools, Saint Louis, Missouri.*

Hon. HENRY KIDDLE, *Superintendent of city-schools, New York, New York.*

Hon. J. W. BULKLEY, *Superintendent of city-schools, Brooklyn, New York.*

Hon. GEORGE B. SEARS, *Superintendent of city-schools, Newark, New Jersey.*

Hon. J. L. PICKARD, *Superintendent of city-schools, Chicago, Illinois.*

Hon. WILLIAM R. CREERY, *Superintendent of city-schools, Baltimore, Maryland.*

Hon. JOHN HANCOCK, *Superintendent of city-schools, Cincinnati, Ohio.*

Hon. A. J. RICKOFF, *Superintendent of city-schools, Cleveland, Ohio.*

Hon. DUANE DOTY, *Superintendent of city-schools, Detroit, Michigan.*

Prof. STEPHENSON, *Superintendent of city-schools, Buffalo, New York.*

Hon. EDWARD SMITH, *Superintendent of city-schools, Syracuse, New York.*

Hon. S. A. ELLIS, *Superintendent of city-schools, Rochester, New York.*

Hon. D. F. DE WOLF, *Superintendent of city-schools, Toledo, Ohio.*

Hon. J. O. WILSON, *Superintendent of city-schools, Washington, District of Columbia.*

Hon. GEORGE H. TINGLEY, *Superintendent of city-schools, Louisville, Kentucky.*

Hon. GEORGE J. LUCKEY, *Superintendent of city-schools, Pittsburg, Pennsylvania.*

Hon. WILLIAM L. DICKINSON, *Superintendent of city-schools, Jersey City, New Jersey.*

Hon. F. C. LAW, *Superintendent of city-schools, Milwaukee, Wisconsin.*

Hon. DANIEL LEACH, *Superintendent of city-schools, Providence, Rhode Island.*

Hon. ARIEL PARISH, *Superintendent of city-schools, New Haven, Connecticut.*

www.ingramcontent.com/pod-product-compliance
Lightning Source LLC
LaVergne TN
LVHW020633110826
845149LV00004B/1166

* 9 7 8 1 4 1 8 1 9 1 4 9 8 *